# America's Role in Revelation Revised

## Eileen Townsend

# TABLE OF CONTENTS

# PREFACE

This book is a revision of the original book, America's Role in Revelation, that I wrote in 2010. Much has happened since then that needed to be clarified and added. What is written in this book will show you America does have an important role to play during the end times spoken of in Revelation.

I will address that role through scriptures, historical facts, and by what is happening in this present time. We, Christians, need to do our part to ensure that God's plans for America are fulfilled. God expects us to take care of what He gives us. My desire is, that the following information will help to increase our knowledge and our understanding concerning the critical time we are living in.

America is in trouble. We, God's people, need to become motivated and take back this special gift He gave us, America. When God gives us a gift, He expects us to protect and care for it. God never intended for the United States of America to get into the shape it is in today. It is our responsibility to recapture this nation and make it one nation under God as it originally was established to be, thanks to our founding fathers.

We are at a pivotal time in our young nation's existence and we must make the decision to fight for this gift that God gave us. It is not too late. We can get our nation back if we Christians and our Jewish brothers get involved. If we step out to do our part in restoring our nation, God will back us up.

There are many scripture references used in this book to validate what I have been shown about the end-time period referred to in Revelation as well as in other areas of the Bible. I prefer to use the King James Version of the Bible whenever possible because it often seems to have a more thorough or complete translation. The Old English Language can be difficult to grasp at times. Because of this, to ensure clarity, I changed to the New International Version when it is obviously saying the exact same thing as the King James Version.

Thank you for reading my book. I pray God will enlighten the truth to you and give you insight into what your role is, in what lies ahead for the world and for this great gift that He gave us, America.

# America's Role in Revelation Revised

# THE BEGINNING

The Bible tells us that there will be a one-world government during the end times. Presently a group of many nations are discussing the possibility of forming an alliance to strengthen the economic and military aspects of their governing powers. Their desire is, that this alliance among them will help with their protection and financial well-being. Even in America, we are hearing rumors that our present government officials are preparing to realign our laws, financial structure, and protections to permit our joining such an alliance. This is not a good choice for our nation to make.

Many nations are very dependent upon other nation's cooperation with the protection for their people and their borders. Financial stability is often linked to trade with other nations. Partnerships between nations can also help to keep up with the fast-changing advancements we are being introduced to almost daily. With all this being true, there is really no need for a centrally controlled government to accomplish this.

That being said, there is still a push to establish one. What is still missing in this present-day scenario, which relates to John's prophecy, is a leader that will unite these nations all together into that one-world government under his influence. That leader has not surfaced yet.

The Bible states knowledge would increase during this time mentioned in Revelation. Our ability to communicate with others has skyrocketed with the introduction of satellites, televisions, cell phones, the internet, artificial intelligence, etc. Add to this, our ability to travel around the world easily, makes our world seem smaller and our personal lives more vulnerable to outside influences.

People are already putting chips under the skin of animals to be able to identify them. It seems to be more acceptable for people to put tattoos on their bodies today than in our nation's past history, particularly among young people. This along with digital markings or codes being required to access entry into many areas, being put on driver's licenses, also being used at places like bank ATMs, or to purchase many items are all preparing the population to easily accept some kind of mark, for identification purposes, to be required. All of this is not just an accident or a chance occurrence.

With as much digital crime and problems of identification the world is having, things are being set up for a world-wide decision that would require everyone to take some kind of identifying mark on their bodies. If things keep progressing at this rate, many of us will be witnesses to what is written in the book of Revelation. This book will help you understand, America does have an important role to play in these end times spoken of in God's word, the Bible.

Even though God is sovereign and self-sufficient, in His great wisdom, He chooses to use people to assist Him in His work on this earth. The Bible states, what was spoken of in Revelation would be sealed until the time of the end. Therefore, we should expect to see more wisdom and knowledge exposed to us about what was written concerning the end times. Especially now that things seem to be lining up with what was written in Revelation. My hope is, the information to follow will help to clarify what is expected of us during our lifetime.

I am going to do my best to share with you what was shown to me about the book of Revelation. It did not come easily or without effort on my part. When God reveals insight to us mere human beings, often it is not that easy to convey. Please bear with me as I show you how it relates to God's word.

The first part of this book will be attempting to explain, through the scriptures, what I was shown about God's relationship with us and the relationship our Father in heaven wants us to have with Him.

This knowledge is a very important aspect for us to understand as it will help us operate in this ever-changing world we live in today. Related to the main topic, it is also needed to help us understand the role that America plays in the book of Revelation. My pray is that you will not take lightly what is revealed in this book.

Since Revelation is mostly based on the visions given to John by God, we will start there.

# JOHN'S VISIONS

The book of Revelation was written by John on the Isle of Patmos. Much, if not all, of what he shared with us in Revelation was revealed to John, by God, through visions. Our Heavenly Father must have considered this information very important because John was commanded, by both God and by Jesus Christ, to write down what was revealed to him in a book and to write personalized letters to be given to the 7 churches in Asia.

> Revelation 1, 1-2: (1) "The revelation of Jesus Christ, which God gave him to show his servants what must soon take place. He made it known by sending his angel to his servant John, (2) who testifies to everything he saw – that is, the word of God and the testimony of Jesus Christ." (NIV)

This shows us that God revealed to His Son, Jesus, what God wanted us, His adopted children, to know about the things that are to happen in the future.

In the following verse we see that God put great emphasis upon this information which He was giving John by stating that those who read and understand the prophecy in this book are blessed.

> Revelation 1, 3: "Blessed is the one who reads the words of this prophecy, and blessed are those who hear it and take to heart what is written in it, because the time is near." (NIV)

There is a stipulation that goes with this message though; the blessed ones must also keep the words of this prophecy.

Our Father is aware of our limitations. He will often give us only a part of what He wants us to do at one time. This is like being handed pieces of a puzzle. Another way that you could understand it, is to see God giving us instructions one step at a time. After a while, all those small pieces of insight or direction that we receive start to unfold into a beautiful plan or picture for us to learn from and to use.

We are then expected to act upon the instruction and wisdom we are given to help bring about what God wants to happen on this earth. In order for us to keep receiving instructions, we must carry out what we were asked to do first.

Revelation plainly states that both God and Jesus spoke to John and commanded him to write down what he saw. Even after God spoke to Jesus about revealing these secrets to John, God decided to stress the importance of the information by speaking to John directly.

In these next few verses John was ordered by God to record in a book what he saw in the visions he was given.

> Revelation 1, 10-11: (10) "I was in the Spirit on the Lord's day, and heard behind me a

great voice, as of a trumpet, (11) Saying, **I am Al'pha and O'me-ga, the first and the last: and, What thou seeth, write in a book, and send** *it* **unto the seven churches which are in A'sia;..."** (KJV)

These verses define themselves as being a statement from our Heavenly Father not only because He identifies Himself as the Alpha and Omega, but also because John describes the voice as coming from behind him.

The Bible tells us that we cannot look upon God's face and live.

Exodus 33, 20: "**But,** He said, **you cannot see my face, for no one may see me and live."** (NIV)

In the above verse, God is speaking with Moses and is explaining why He, God, cannot show Moses His face.

Moses had a special relationship with God as described in several places of the Bible. In the verse below is an example of this special relationship.

Palms 106, 23: "Therefore He said that He would destroy them, had not Moses His chosen stood before Him in the breach, to turn away His wrath, lest He should destroy them." (NIV)

As you can see, God turned away His wrath because of what Moses did.

In these next 2 verses, John was overwhelmed at seeing Jesus. Jesus reassured John of who He is and not to be afraid. Remember, John walked and talked with Jesus before He suffered and died on the cross so John knew who Jesus was. John saw Him die on that cross. I am sure this was a lot for John to take in.

> Revelation 1, 17-18: (17) "When I saw him, I fell at his feet as though dead. Then he placed his right hand on me and said: **Do not be afraid. I am the First and the Last.** (18) **I am the Living One; I was dead, and behold I am alive for ever and ever! And I hold the keys of death and Hades.**" (NIV)

This clearly defines the speaker as Jesus Christ. He came to earth to die so that the price for our sins could be paid. Jesus then gave John instructions on what was to be written in letters to the 7 churches.

As the Bible tells us – because of what Jesus suffered, we now can be forgiven of the sins we have committed and be cleansed in Jesus's blood which was shed for the removal of our sins.

> Matthew 26, 28: **"For this is My blood of the new testament, which is shed for many for the remission of sins."** (KJV)

After hearing the words from God and being instructed by Jesus, John was given visions. He then attempted to put into writing what he was shown. This is not always as easy as it may seem.

When God gives insight to His servants and children, we are limited by what we are capable of doing, our present knowledge on the subject, and what we are capable of understanding. John was attempting to write down what he saw, to explain things and events that he was shown in the visions.

This included things that were to happen in his present time as well as what was to happen in a future time.

> Revelation 1, 19: **"Write the things which thou hast seen, and the things which are, and the things which shall be hereafter;"** (KJV)

This could not have been easy for John or for anyone to do.

Our Heavenly Father wants all of His people, those living then, His people living now, and for His people who are not born yet, to hear and understand this book of Revelation. God stressed the importance of the words and visions that He was about to give John by God speaking with him personally and by having Jesus instruct John as well.

God told us He would be revealing the truth of what John wrote in Revelation at the time of the end. Now is the time for us to understand these end-time visions, that were revealed by God, about what will happen as well as what part He expects us to have in it. The Bible states that during this end-time period wisdom and knowledge will increase. We are seeing that increase in almost all aspects of human life today.

We need to understand that many of the pictures John saw were of things which had not been seen before by him or by anyone else living in that day and time. This would make it difficult for John to put into writing what he saw. How would you describe war ships, machines, jet aircrafts, bombs, guns, tanks, televisions, cell phones, and many other things, which are common in today's world, if you had never seen anything like that before? That would not be an easy task for anyone to carry out.

Much of what is written in Revelation has been misunderstood or often seemed just too difficult to comprehend. Because of this, many people have ignored it or they have just given up on understanding what is written in the book of Revelation. We need to try to understand what God is saying, as it appears many of us will be living during the time spoken of in Revelation. No time in recorded history has things lined up with what was revealed to us in God's book like it is now.

God spoke to Daniel about the end times as well. This verse refers to Daniel's request for understanding of what God had just revealed to him.

> Daniel 12, 4: "**But thou, O Dan'iel, shut up the words, and seal the book,** *even* **to the**

**time of the end: many shall run to and fro, and knowledge shall be increased.**" (KJV)

We not only need to understand what is written in the Bible about the end times, we also need to see what our responsibility is in being sure God's plans are fulfilled. God choses to use His people to do this.

We, God's children, should expect to experience personal increase in our understanding and new insight to be given to us, by God, during this time. We must not be consumed by our own personal problems, responsibilities, and daily lives to ignore what is happening to our nation and in our world. We must be aware of what is going on and help to prevent evil plans from being fulfilled. Our Father in heaven always keeps His word and His promises.

If you are 50 years old or older, you have experienced in your lifetime a great deal of new ideas, new developments, and new inventions. This increase in knowledge has totally changed our lifestyle from previous generations and increased the need for us to keep up with all these new changes. This is both good and bad. Although these new gadgets, medicines, inventions, and ways of doing things have helped us in many ways, they also have created situations that are often difficult for us to handle.

With the increase in knowledge also comes increased responsibility. The pressures of life now are often too great for many people to cope with. The added stress on people's lives causes physical, mental, and emotional changes which often result in strange or inappropriate behavior. We are seeing the results of excessive stress every day in our communities, in the daily news reports, as well as in our very own families. Things are changing so fast that it is hard to keep up with all of the new information and new developments. If we ever needed God to be a part of our lives, we really do need His direction now.

When things start to become more than we can handle, we generally start pulling back and focusing on things closer to home and family. I call this the ostrich effect. If you bury your head in the sand, like the old cliché states that the ostriches do when afraid, this only makes you think you are safe. In all actuality the tender-most parts of your anatomy are left exposed and vulnerable to the very dangers you refuse to face. That is what many people, including Americans, are doing right now.

It is obvious that Revelation was inspired by God and passed down from generation to generation for the purpose of instructing, informing, preparing, and giving insight to His adopted children as well as to all those who would venture to read His book, the Bible.

Our Heavenly Father wants us to be aware and prepared for what is to happen during this time. He wants us to receive the understanding of what is contained in this end-time prophecy so we will not be taken by surprise. God put a great deal of effort into being sure we would be aware of what is to come so we can be prepared to do our part in these events, as they unfold right before our eyes.

God did this, so we can resist the evil of this age and be the light He needs us to be amid the darkness that is present now and is yet to come. He wants us to have a relationship with Him while on this earth as well as having everyone in heaven with Him. Our Heavenly Father does things to help people recognize their need for Him and to help all of us realize His willingness to be involved in our lives. That is why He gave us the Bible, His word. God always defends, protects, and provides for His obedient children.

# GOD'S LOVE FOR US

We are loved by God. I know we often do not feel His love. Many times, we do not feel we deserve His caring attention because of the choices we make in life. That is correct. We do not deserve His love, but God loves us anyway. It is very important that we understand His love for us, so we can go through this life with the confidence and assurance of His devotion to us. It is essential that we understand His willingness to assist us in this life. That confidence will enable us to do things we may never have dreamed we could possibly accomplish.

America is nothing on its own. America is derived of We the People and the actions we do. If we expect America to stay great and accomplish what God expects of it, we must take the actions required to bring that about. We can do everything that He is expecting us to do, with His help. We are not alone in this life unless we choose to be alone. He is ever present to assist us in accomplishing things we could not do by ourselves. We must seek to have a good relationship with God just as Moses did. The choice to do this is more beneficial than you may realize.

Our understanding of our Father's love for us is also very important for our ability to comprehend the book of Revelation. Much of what was written in Revelation was not to be understood until the time was right for that knowledge to be given.

It appears, by what is happening in our world today, it is coming close to that period of time spoken of in Revelation. We need to be confident in His love and His willingness to assist us, as individuals, so we can carry out the tasks He sets before us. God goes before us to prepare the way so, if we cooperate with His plan – everything falls into place as we walk through it.

This biblical quote is Moses talking with God and asking to see His glory.

> Exodus 33, 18-20: (18) "Then Moses said, Now show me your glory. (19) And the LORD said, **I will cause all my goodness to pass in front of you, and I will proclaim my name, the LORD, in your presence. I will have mercy on whom I will have mercy, and I will have compassion on whom I will have compassion.** (20) **But,** He said, **you cannot see my face, for no one may see me and live**." (NIV)

Our Heavenly Father states here that He cannot show His face to us or we will die.

Moses spent a lot of time in the presence of God and wanted to see what He looked like. God graciously accommodated Moses in a way God could without hurting him. Moses developed a special relationship with God because he spent time with Him and was willing to do as God requested.

We can develop a special or personal relationship with our Heavenly Father as well. We become adopted children of God because of what Jesus did for us. Jesus spent His life on this earth showing us how we are to live then gave up His life, in an agonizing manner, on the cross so that the sins we commit will be forgiven.

Because Jesus paid the price needed for us to be forgiven of the sins we commit, we can now have a relationship with God, His Father. God wants a relationship with all of us and has made it possible for us to have that. It is all up to us. We can make that choice to use what Jesus did for us. When we do, then we can choose how much of a relationship we want to have with God.

Our Father in Heaven must think people are very special because, He spoke into existence everything else except for Adam and Eve. Genesis states God formed Adam from the dust of the earth.

> Genesis 2, 7: "the LORD God formed the man from the dust of the ground and breathed into his nostrils the breath of life, and the man became a living being." (NIV)

This tells us that God put more effort into the creation of our bodies, which are used to carry our spirits throughout the life that He gave us, then He did with any other thing that He created.

He then blew His own breath into the body, that He formed with His own hands, to give life to it. We must be very special to God for Him to focus so much attention to the details of the physical container as well as using His own breath to bring life into it. Our Heavenly Father did not put that much effort into the creation of anything else. That verse is an example of how much care God put into the creation of man. We are special to Him.

These next verses give us more insight into the loving care God wants to give us. God goes on to say to Moses:

> Exodus 33, 22-23: (22) **"When my glory passes by, I will put you in a cleft in the rock and cover you with my hand until I have passed by. (23) Then I will remove my hand and you will see my back; but my face must not be seen**." (NIV)

Our Heavenly Father cared for Moses so much, that He did not trust that Moses would keep his eyes shut and not try to look upon God's face.

To ensure the safety of him, God put His hand over Moses to protect him so no damage would be done to Moses. Our Father in heaven wanted to ensure Moses's safety even if he chose to disobeyed what God had told him to do. This shows us how much God cares for His people as well as what a loving and protective nature our Heavenly Father has toward us.

God does care about us and He desires to be a part of our lives. He seeks after our love and attention just as a good earthly father seeks the love and attention from his children. God wants to teach and care for us so we can live out our lives in such a manner, that when it is time for us to leave this earth, we can join Him in heaven.

That is why God gave us His word, the Bible, so we will know by examples, the best way to live out our lives on this earth. God wants us to make a positive difference in this world and to have every opportunity to obtain a special place with Him in heaven. I don't know how you feel about that, but I personally do not want to disappoint Him. I am looking forward to being with my Father in heaven.

Because of what Jesus did, we can now be under His protective covering. We can do what He says we can do. We can develop a personal relationship with Him and with God. What Jesus did makes us the adopted children of our Heavenly Father with all its privileges and its responsibilities.

The more we seek after God, the more He rewards us with blessings and insight. The more time we spend with God in prayer and just talking with Him, the better we get to know Him. This personal relationship with God will also help us discover His way of doing things.

This is very similar to us spending time with other people we have become friends with on this earth. The more time we spend with a person – the more we learn about them and the more we become attached to them. It is the same with God, only better.

God is giving us more insight here:

> Revelation 3, 18: "**I counsel you to buy from me gold refined in the fire, so you can become rich; and white clothes to wear, so you can cover your shameful nakedness; and salve to put on your eyes, so you can see.**" (NIV)

God is challenging us to seek after the better things in this life, the things that will bring us everlasting joy and blessings.

Our Father is using the word "buy" here. This addresses the fact that not all things are just given to us. Somethings are precious enough that there needs to be a price paid to receive it. We can always go to our Heavenly Father in Jesus's name and request the knowledge we will need to receive what we are asking for. God would not have stated this if He did not intend to answer us.

More life direction given to us by our loving Heavenly Father.

> Revelation 3, 19: "**Those whom I love I rebuke and discipline. So be earnest, and repent.**" (NIV)

Our Father in heaven is telling us here that He will shape and mold us into people that can be used by Him.

Just as a soldier is shaped and molded in boot camp to prepare for the battles he must be involved in, so will God structure our experiences and bring people into our lives that will prepare us for events that we must face in the future.

We must look to our Heavenly Father for direction so we will not miss out on the little clues and events, that He is sending our way, to prepare us for the future He has planned for our lives. We must also seek the wisdom we will need to be sure we are not deceived. God wants us to know the truth.

Jesus is the one speaking here:

> Revelation 3, 20-21: (20) **"Here I am! I stand at the door and knock. If anyone hears my voice and opens the door, I will come in and eat with him, and he with me.** (21) **To him who overcomes, I will give the right to sit with me on my throne, just as I overcame and sat down with my Father on his throne."** (NIV)

Jesus is asking all of us to let Him into our hearts and lives. He stands and waits for our response because He truly wants to have a relationship with us. Jesus loves us so much that He wants us to walk out our lives with Him. Jesus is the key that allows us to have a relationship with God. Jesus is also giving us some insight into the rewards we will receive for accomplishing what is asked of us during our lifetime.

This statement is given to us to stress the importance of what was just said in the previous 2 verses.

> Revelation 3, 22: **"He who has an ear, let him hear what the Spirit says to the churches."** (NIV)

God is sending us a "pay attention" message.

Jesus suffered and died so that we can enter into a personal relationship with Him and our Heavenly Father. Jesus wants to lead and guide us through this life. As any good leader would do – He will teach, correct, and do what is necessary to prepare us so we can face the problems and tasks we must encounter during our time on this earth. In this life Jesus states, the ones who overcome the evil that they must face will sit with Him in heaven. What an honor that would be!!!

Jesus allows us, God's adopted children, to go to God directly and ask for understand and direction. He will hear us and answer our prayers. I hope all God's children who read this book, will go to God and ask for His truth and insight about what is written in it. We need to find out what our Father wants us to do to help bring about His will on earth. Do not forget, God often gives us insight piece by piece.

Here are some more verses to helps us understand God's love for us.

> Matthew 7, 7-8: (7) **"Ask and it will be given to you; seek and you will find; knock and the door will be opened to you.** (8) **For everyone who asks receives; he who seeks finds; and to him who knocks, the door will be opened"** (NIV)

This is Jesus telling us that we need to keep trying even if things do not come easily to us at first. Some things come to us by asking, some take a little more effort, and sometimes we may have to hunt for the answer. Jesus is also saying if we keep trying, we will have the reward we deserve. God loves us. He will guide us through what has to happen for us to receive what we need – if we don't give up. This process also helps us learn more about His way of doing things. That, in itself, is a precious reward.

Jesus goes on to tell us, through examples like He often did, about God's love for us.

> Matthew 7, 9-11: (9) "**Which of you, if his son asks for bread, will give him a stone?** (10) **Or if he asks for a fish, will give him a snake?** (11) **If you, then, though you are evil, know how to give good gifts to your children, how much more will your Father in heaven give good gifts to those who ask him!**" (NIV)

Again, Jesus is inviting us to ask God for help with the issues and decisions we need to make in this life.

This states that God considers us His children and He wants to give good things to us. If our Father in heaven loves us so much, how then can we believe He would leave us, His children, unprotected especially in a time of trouble? These verses also show us how much Jesus and God want to be part of our lives.

Wise people will do what is required of them so they can obtain the relationship with God that is needed. They then can ask Him for the direction, wisdom, and understanding that they will need to be successful in the important things in life. Especially for the understanding needed to prevent them from being deceived by anyone.

Jesus spoke of a time when we will be able to understand plainly those things that He told us about God.

> John 16, 24-27: (24) **"Until now you have not asked for anything in my name. Ask and you will receive, and your joy will be complete. (25) Though I have been speaking figuratively, a time is coming when I will no longer use this kind of language but will tell you plainly about my Father. (26) In that day you will ask in my name. I am not saying that I will ask the Father on your behalf. (27) No, the Father**

**himself loves you because you have loved me and have believed that I came from God."** (NIV)

This passage again tells us of God's love for us. Jesus is our connection – He states that we do not have to go through Him with our requests. Jesus gave us permission to go to God directly by the use of Jesus's name.

We are no longer in need of a physical high priest to go to God for us as the Jewish people do. Jesus is our High Priest. God's Jewish children, who are under the Old Testament laws and rules, need a high priest to go to God for them. Once we accept Jesus as our personal Lord and Savior – He is our High Priest. He gave us permission to go to our Father in heaven directly by using Jesus's name.

Jesus told us that God loves us because we believe in Jesus and that He was sent to us by God. If God truly loves us, He will do what is best for us – His children. If our Heavenly Father knows trouble is coming, He will give His people the knowledge needed to overcome that trouble.

It is our job to respond to that knowledge and take the action needed to prevent the problems, that God is warning us about, from occurring. We are His instruments on this earth to bring about the blessings in this life that He has planned for us as well as helping God bless others.

In John 17, are the recordings of what Jesus said to His disciples right before He went into the garden of Gethsemane. He is trying to share with them part of what His sacrifice on the cross would mean for them and for all of us. He is also speaking with His Father in these verses to follow.

This is Jesus speaking with God, His Father.

> John 17, 15-16: (15) **"My prayer is not that you take them out of the world but that you protect them from the evil one.** (16) **They are not of the world, even as I am not of it."** (NIV)

Here Jesus is asking the Father to keep us on this earth and to protect us from evil. Again, this shows us that we, Christians, will have God's protection. Jesus is also stating that we are not of the evil in this world just as He is not.

Jesus goes on to say:

> John 17, 17-18: (17) **"Sanctify them by the truth; your word is truth.** (18) **As you sent me into the world, I have sent them into the world."** (NIV)

He is stating here that we are to be sanctified through the truth of God's word. Jesus also is stating that we are to live our lives in this world as He lived His.

The old adage, the truth will set you free, really applies here. Jesus showed us how we are to live out our lives on this earth. We are to influence others as Jesus's life influenced ours. The way we live should draw others to seek after what we have through Jesus. What we do should inspire others to join us by doing their part in bringing about God's plans. If we cooperate with what God wants, amazing things will happen.

There is always a sense of peace when we know the right thing to do and then we decide to do it. Just as Jesus was sent to this earth to save us, He is sending us into the world to spread God's truth and for us to protect what He gave us. When we do it, others may see our good works and also seek after that special relationship we have developed with God.

Jesus further explains what He is giving to us believers:

> John 17, 19- 20: (19) **"For them I sanctify myself, that they too may be truly sanctified. (20) My prayer is not for them alone. I pray also for those who will believe in me through their message,"** (NIV)

He was sanctified and was made one with His Father. Jesus asked God to sanctify those who were present with Him at that time as well as to sanctify all that will believe in Jesus through God's word.

In the following verse, He also requested that we be made one with Him and God. Jesus was making all people who would believe in Him and do the things we are asked to do, to be part of His family in heaven.

We can see this by what Jesus said in this following verse:

> John 17, 21: "**that all of them may be one, Father, just as you are in me and I am in you. May they also be in us so that the world may believe that you have sent Me.**" (NIV)

Jesus is telling us that God the Father dwells within Jesus. God can now also dwell within us because Jesus suffered and died on the cross to pay the price for our sins. Jesus is giving us permission to become part of His Heavenly Family. This is a powerful statement and a gift we have been given.

God loves all His creation but He took extra care in creating people. Our Heavenly Father wishes He could give guidance to all people; but to the people who have accepted Jesus as their personal Savior, God has given them more privileges, more anointing, and more attention because of what Jesus did for us. Do not be deceived. Remember, the guidance that the Holy Spirit gives us will never contradict God's word, the Bible.

Some people call the direction that is given to us as being from the Holy Spirit, our conscience, our instinct, or guidance from the Spirit of God. No matter what you call it, this is the job of the Holy Spirit of God, to guide and direct us so that we can make a difference with our lives and show our Father in heaven's love on this earth. Jesus wants us to stay plugged into that heavenly hotline for help with all our daily needs and instructions. He wants to help us overcome the problems we will face and to help us carry out the tasks we will be given to do.

This awareness, and the ability to recognize it, is developed over time as well as with the attention we give to spending time with God. Our gateway to being able to do all this, is asking for forgiveness of our sins in Jesus's name.

If all God's children could be and do what God designed for us to be and do, we would truly experience heaven on this earth. If we would pay attention to what the Bible is telling us, seek God's direction for our lives, and do what is asked of us – this world would be a much better place to live in.

We, who have accepted Jesus as our personal Savior, have many privileges and responsibilities. We can go to God in Jesus's name and receive forgiveness for the sins we commit. We then can request blessings, healings, and wisdom from our Heavenly Father and He will give us much of what we ask for. All of this requires a relationship with Jesus for it to be accomplished.

As any good earthly father would do, we should expect God to say "no" to us now and again since not everything we ask for is good for us. Even when we get the no answers, God often will give us some insight on the subject or another path to take. It is not uncommon, if we stay open to what He is showing us, that He will also create events that will head us in the right direction for a better way to handle our requests. It will not be so easy for us to be misled, if we are familiar with our Heavenly Father's way of doing things. Spending time with Him and doing what He asks, is the best way for us to accomplish that.

Jesus went on to say:

> John 17, 22-23: (22) **"I have given them the glory that you gave me, that they may be one as we are one: (23) I in them and you in me. May they be brought to complete unity to let the world know that you sent me and have loved them even as you have loved me.**" (NIV)

This is a very intense statement Jesus is making here. Jesus is saying that He is passing down much of what God has given Him so that we, Christians, can be one with God and Him.

We must accept Jesus as Savior, be sanctified, and receive His glory in order for us to be allowed to become part of God's adopted family. If we can perfect this closeness with both Jesus and with God, we then can be used by God. When we do this, we can become part of His miracle-working power and presence on this earth. This is possible for all God's children to achieve, if we are willing to make the effort to become the person our Father in heaven desires us to be. There is no better or more rewarding position for us to be in.

Jesus continues speaking with God here:

> John 17, 24-26: (24) **"Father, I want those you have given me to be with me where I am, and to see my glory, the glory you have given me because you loved me before the creation of the world.** (25) **Righteous Father, though the world does not know you, I know you, and they know that you have sent me.** (26) **I have made you known to them, and will continue to make you known in order that the love you have for me may be in them and that I myself may be in them."** (NIV)

This seems to be more of a private prayer between Jesus and the Father. Jesus is elaborating on His request to extend the rights and privileges that Jesus enjoys as God's Son, to us who believe in Him.

Jesus in part, is speaking to Himself here, to build Himself up because of what He was about to suffer as well as for all of us to understand the importance of what His suffering meant for us. Our Savior was preparing Himself to start the process of giving up His life by surrendering Himself into the hands of the evil of that time and ending His life by a torturous death on the cross for the payment of our sins.

In the garden of Gethsemane, Jesus was given time alone with His Father to prepare for what was about to happen. He was preparing to suffer greatly and die an agonizing death, that He did not deserve, to pay the price for our sins. Jesus had to first surrender His will over to His Father so Jesus could bear the suffering He must go through. I am sure His stress level was incredible.

Can you imagine what Jesus was going through? He had the right to say no, I will not do this. He had the same free will to make choices for His life, just like we do today. If Jesus had caved in, as many of us do when we are under pressure, and had decided to cancel His appointment with the cross – can you imagine what this world would be like today?

I hope you understand what making that decision would mean for all the people on this earth. One fact is a sure thing; heaven would be a much lonelier place as most of us would not be able to enter heaven because of the choices we made while on this earth. Jesus truly does deserve our praise and our obedience.

We, God's adopted children, need to seek wisdom and understanding to be given to us so we will be able to do what is necessary to fulfill the tasks our Father in heaven expects us to do. We can see the Bible unfolding before our eyes and we will be held accountable to God for what we individually do, especially during this very important time in history. God chooses to use us to help bring about His will on this earth. His wise children will seek their Heavenly Father's help and direction to be able to accomplish His expectations of them.

We do have an enemy that will do his best to try and prevent God's plan from being completed. Our job is to make sure that does not happen. If we seek God's direction for how we can do this, He will guide us along the path we need to take to accomplish it. Just as Jesus accepted His job – so should we accept ours.

We all have a part in bringing about His will on this earth. In this present time, saving America from becoming part of the one-world government is the job all of us have to do. We are responsible and accountable for our actions.

Do not worry about what others are doing. God can and will raise up people to help us accomplish what needs to be done. If we take our focus away from the tasks we are given, it will only interfere in our ability to carry out our part in these end-time requirements. Distraction is a common tactic the enemy uses to prevent us from accomplishing what God asks us to do. A wise person will not lose focus on his responsibilities and disappoint God.

Forgive me for getting a head of myself. I have not yet shown you the leadership position God has planned for America to do during these end times. America dose play an important role in God's plans spoken of in Revelation – as I hope to prove to you in the following chapters.

# CHRISTIANS IN REVELATION

There are references to Christians present in the book of Revelation. First, I needed to show you the verses in the Bible that express the love and protection we have as God's adopted children. This was needed in order to help verify what I am about to share with you in this book.

Here is one of the descriptions John gave us of God's people which will be involved in the end-time battle. If you notice, these verses are referring to only a select group of Jewish people.

> Revelation 7, 2-4: (2) "And I saw another angel ascending from the east, having the seal of the living God: and he cried with a loud voice to the four angels, to whom it was given to hurt the earth and the sea, (3) Saying, hurt not the earth, neither the sea, nor the trees, till we have sealed the servants of our God in their foreheads. (4) And I heard the number of them which were sealed: *and there were* sealed a hundred *and* forty *and* four thousand of all the tribes of the children of Is'ra-el." (KJV)

Since there is no mention of any other nationalities other than the Jewish people and those 144,000 Jewish men who were sealed by God for this event, this would suggest that there were very few if any Christians present there. The area described in these above verses is most likely the battle zone.

These next two verses from Revelation are describing the vision John saw of the sealed Jewish servants in Heaven after the battle was won in Israel by Jesus's return. These men were virgins, they were selected and protected, who did the will of God.

Here, our Heavenly Father gives us more insight on the sealed servants.

> Revelation 14, 3-4: "And they sung as it were a song before the throne, and before the four beasts, and the elders: and no man could learn that song but the hundred *and* forty *and* four thousand, which were redeemed from the earth. (4) These are they which were not defiled with women; for they are virgins. These are they which follow the Lamb whithersoever He goeth. These were redeemed from among men, *being* the first fruits unto God and to the Lamb." (KJV)

This is what is happening in Heaven after Jesus has won the battle against the beast. Jesus is now sitting on His throne in heaven and He now holds control over the earth. These selected Jewish men now know who Jesus really is and are dedicated to Him. He is their true Messiah.

We can see that these sealed servants are a very special group of men, chosen from each one of the twelve tribes of the Jewish people. They are handpicked, dedicated to serving God and Jesus. This select group are virgins, and were marked by God the Father for the end-time battle. They have completed the job they were assigned to do. In the above verses, God is speaking of the role these sealed servants of God will have in heaven. It states they follow Jesus wherever He goes.

This select group of Jewish men are not the ones referred to, in the Bible, as being written in the Lamb's Book of Life. The one's written in this book are those who have chosen Jesus as their personal Savior. The New Testament refers to these people as being Christians.

God gave different rules that the Jewish people are to follow in order to be accepted by Him in heaven. This was given to them thousands of years before Jesus sacrificed His life for us. These rules did not allow them the same privileges we share, that Jesus gave us, unless they too accept Him as their Lord and Savior. They do not have the same right to go directly to God as we can through Jesus.

The Bible does show us there are Christians around at this time because of what is written in the following verse as well as in other biblical verses. Revelation 13 is addressing and describing a beast, which is not a single man as much as an army of men, that the dragon uses to try and destroy what God holds dear to His heart – the Jewish people.

God loves us, but because He is a just God, He must condemn the actions that go against His righteous will as well as those people who will not repent. This chapter and verse is referring to the anti-christ being worshiped by people who are not written in the Lamb's Book of Life.

> Revelation 13, 8: "And all that dwell upon the earth shall worship him, whose names are not written in the book of life of the Lamb slain from the foundation of the world." (KJV)

John states here that all people shall worship the anti-christ except the people in the Lamb's book.

The above passage states that there are people present during this time, who will not worship the anti-christ or take part in the one-world government. These people must also believe in Jesus because they are written in His book. The Lamb's book contains people who have accepted that Jesus died for their sins and they accepted Him as their High Priest. In order to be written in Jesus's book, you must recognize Him as your Lord and Savior. Therefore, every time the Bible refers to people who are written in the Lamb's book, it is speaking of Christians since they are the people who have accepted Jesus as their personal Lord and Savior.

That distinction is given to people who do this no matter what tribe or nationality they come from.

Here is another reference to Christians being present at this time.

> Revelation 12, 11: "And they overcame him by the blood of the Lamb, and by the word of their testimony; and they loved not their lives unto death." (KJV)

So, whenever we see the Bible referring to the people written in the Lamb's Book of Life, this must be referring to Christians. They are the only people who have the right to overcome anything by the blood of the Lamb. They are those who have taken Jesus as Savior.

Both these previously mentioned passages in Revelation clearly mention people, present during this time, who are Christians. A third passage to consider is:

> Revelation 12, 17: "And the dragon was wroth with the woman, and went to make war with the remnant of her seed, which keep the commandments of God, and have the testimony of Je'sus Christ." (KJV)

This quote from the Bible also refers to those who have the testimony of Jesus.

This verse cannot be referring to Jewish people, as a whole, because at this time they do not believe Jesus is their Messiah. They do not accept Jesus as anything other than a prophet. Jewish people cannot have His testimony unless they have accepted Jesus as Savior. Once again, the Bible is putting Christians present somewhere on the earth and the beast goes to make war with them. If the beast, led by the dragon, went somewhere to make war with these Christians – then they must be gathered in a different place.

Christians have more privileges and rights because of what Jesus did for us than the Jewish people do. Our Jewish brothers are the apple of God's eye. Jesus came from a Jewish birth line – from the birth line of King David and they are God's chosen people. Although God loves both the Christians and the Jewish people, each in their own special way, there is a difference.

The Jewish children of God are still under the Old Testament law. They cannot pray directly to God, our Father in heaven, until a sacrifice is given up for their sins. Once we ask for forgiveness in Jesus's name, He is our sacrifice, we are immediately back under grace. We, Christians, are under grace because of what Jesus did for us.

Although Christians are still under God's laws, when we break His laws or commit sin, we can ask for forgiveness in the name of Jesus, then all our privileges and rights are returned to us. When God's Jewish children commit sin or break His laws, they must go to their Jewish high priest with an animal to sacrifice. The price for their sin is symbolically handled by the killing of that animal. This was meant to be a symbol or an example for them to see in reference to what Jesus would do for all mankind. These animal sacrifices will once again return, when the rebuilding of the temple is completed in Jerusalem.

Another difference Christians have is that we are from all nations and people. There are Jewish Christians as well. The only real distinction we Christians have, from the rest of the world, is that we have accepted what Jesus did for us. We have accepted Him as Savior.

Even today most of the Jewish people, who are under the Old Testament law, if they accept Jesus as anyone special at all – it is only as a prophet. They do not accept Him as Savior and they do not have His testimony.

God takes good care of both His adopted children and His servants. This passage in Revelation shows God's protection for His sealed servants.

> Revelation 9, 3-6: (3) "And there came out of the smoke locusts upon the earth: and unto them was given power, as the scorpions of the earth have power. (4) And it was commanded them that they should not hurt the grass of the earth, neither any green thing, neither any tree; but only those men which have not the

seal of God in their foreheads. (5) And to them it was given that they should not kill them, but that they should be tormented five months: and their torment *was* as the torment of a scorpion, when he striketh a man." (6) And in those days shall men seek death, and shall not find it: and shall desire to die, and death shall flee from them. (KJV)

This also implies that the believers in Jesus Christ were not around this area.

Remember, the sealed servants are only the 144,000 Jewish men set aside by God for the fulfillment of the end-time prophecy. There is no mention of the people written in the Lamb's book of life in this passage. Once again, the Bible is putting Christians present somewhere else on this earth during this time mentioned in Revelation.

Do you think God would allow His adopted children to suffer when He goes to such great lengths to protect His servants? I do not believe our Father in Heaven would do that. God, who loves us, has a place somewhere on the earth designed to protect the people that have become His adopted children. We are not in the area described in the end-time battle. But the Bible clearly puts us here on this earth during that time – where are we?

Since the Bible states that God has decided to leave Christians on this earth, during this important but troubled time on our planet, we must be protected just as our Father has protected His Jewish chosen ones. We, Christians, must not be in the area that is to suffer the plagues involved in this end-time war. Our Heavenly Father must have prepared a safe place for us to be in, somewhere else on this earth.

# THE WHOLE EARTH

We are looking through the eyes of a man, John, who was trying to describe what he saw in visions given to him by God. God then ordered him to write down in a book what he was shown. Both God and Jesus instructed John to then send it, along with personalized letters, to the 7 churches in Asia. Our Father in Heaven was showing John what was to happen in the areas on this earth that he, John, was familiar with. These areas described in the book of Revelation are the land of Israel and the nearby territories.

When John is describing the earth he saw in his visions, he is speaking from his own limited understanding about our planet called "earth". Here is an example:

> Revelation 7, 1: "And after these things I saw four angels standing on the four corners of the earth, holding the four winds of the earth, that the wind should not blow on the earth, nor on the sea, nor on any tree." (KJV)

The statement, "...standing on the four corners of the earth," implies that John must have believed that the earth has corners.

Today we now realize our earth is round; it does not have any corners. Do not forget, in the ancient-time period that John was living in, most people believed our earth was flat. Many people back then, did not travel far from where they were born and raised so their wisdom of what existed past what they could see was very limited.

Historically, we can see the belief that John expresses some people, even at a later time period, had because of what ancient maps and information about that time have shown us. We should be able to understand a little better what John is trying to say here, if we take into account his understanding of what our planet consisted of. Realizing this, should change our understanding and outlook on what he is trying to tell us.

If you understand, what John was saying to us was coming from his limited knowledge of what our planet really consists of, we can view his writings in a different light. So, in John's understanding, he sees an angel at each end of that vision. He believes what he was seeing in his visions is the whole earth. John was writing down what he observed, using his limited understanding of what he knew about the subject. John only saw areas of the earth that he personally knew about.

Even people who did more extensive traveling, and lived in the areas described by John, were apparently not aware of the land mass we currently call America. Since travel across open sea was so difficult, and many also believed that the earth was flat, most sailors would not leave sight of land unless they knew for sure, there was land in the direction that they were headed. Many believed if they did not do that – they could fall off the end of the earth.

At that time, if people chose to travel by sea, they would follow the coastline to go wherever they wanted to go. There is no historical evidence that the people back then, were aware there was a large mass of land farther out to sea which contained the area we now call America. Even if John knew the earth was round, (although that does not seem likely by what he wrote) I am sure by what we have learned about that time in history, he was not aware that a second continent containing the land we inhabit, America, existed.

Here is a website address, in Wikipedia, that takes you to maps and information of the known world at about the time John would have received these visions. Some of these examples of maps were of times both before and after John wrote his part in Revelations.

https://en.wikipedia.org/wiki/Early_world_maps

Since what John saw consisted of his entire knowledge of what was contained on the earth, he called earth in the visions "the whole earth". What

God revealed to John was events happening in the land of Israel and its surrounding territories that were involved in the pursuit of destroying Israel.

Another aspect we should factor into all of this is, the beast that is attacking Israel is described as being built of many heads, horns, and kings without a reference as to where it came from. Since the land where all this is happening seems to be within the areas John is familiar with – why did he not mention the name or place it came from? Could the beast be coming from lands that he is not aware of?

I do not have the answer to that. The important part of this is, none of the descriptions of the end-time battle given to us by John includes lands outside of his knowledge. This is not a description of this happening to the entire world that we know of today.

I have searched the book of Revelation, and other parts of the Bible that relate to these end-time events, to try to find any mention of a land mass which includes this second continent, especially the land we call America. There is no mention of this second continent, that I could find, in any description of the lands that were attacking the Jewish people in Israel. In conclusion – John's whole earth in reality is truly only, at most, about half of our planet called "earth".

I hope you can see that John's whole earth really is not the entire planet. The fact that I was not able to find any mention of this second continent anywhere in the Bible made me very curious. All of these unanswered questions caused me to seek God for those answers.

I truly believe John labored to describe what he had been shown in the visions. I have no doubts that he did his best, with the knowledge that he possessed, to write down what he saw. God, Himself, told us He prevented the understanding of these visions, to be given to John or anyone else, until the time of the end.

That is why we should expect to be given more understanding and insight about these end-time events at this present time. This should help to relieve many Christians of the belief that we have no choice but to allow the whole world to be taken over by the anti-christ. A loving father would never do that to the children he loves. Why then would we believe God would do that to the children He loves.

God chooses to use people to do His work on this earth. That is a gift He gives us. When you have received knowledge from someone whose wisdom and understanding is way above your own, it is often difficult to share what you have learned.

This is even more true when you have been given insight from God.

We often cannot totally express to others what He shows us. This is because we are limited in our ability to transfer information in the same depth that it is given to us.

God understands our limitations and will work with us as long as we are willing to cooperate with Him. It is our job to seek His help in understanding what He had hidden in this book of Revelation and take the action required to bring about what God intends to happen.

There are many areas on earth that are not present in the description John shares with us. Even in Daniel's accounting of his end-time visions, there is no description of lands outside of the areas described in the book of Revelation.

Therefore, how can we assume that the whole earth, as we know it today, is controlled by the beast or the anti-christ? John's description of the whole earth really is not the entire land mass called "earth".

This realization is important for us to have as it will impact what we do during these end times.

America does not need to, nor should we, join that one-world government that is described in the Bible. We must take the action required to stop our leaders from joining the nations that are now trying to form a one-world government – no matter how well it is presented as being beneficial to us.

It is unfortunately normal for government leadership to put unfavorable products in pretty packaging to sell us on an idea they know we may have objection too. Do not be deceived into believing joining this world government will be a good thing for America to do. It will not be.

# THE ANTI-CHRIST

The anti-christ is often spoken of as this overpowering, all-consuming individual who is able to completely captivate and mesmerize the entire world. Also, that he and his partners in crime seem to be able to influence the entire planet to join their side in overtaking the small nation of Israel. I have always had a problem with this projected image of the anti-christ, or anyone for that matter, who is influenced or controlled by satan.

I know what we, God's children, can do with our Father in heaven's help. I know that my Heavenly Father is much stronger, bigger, and wiser than anyone. He can handle anyone or anything that presents a problem. I also know that He certainly can handle whatever satan can dish out. God wants His children to complete the tasks required to keep His will functioning properly on this earth. It is our job to discover what He wants us to do to make sure His will happens and then do it.

The verses to follow are referring to the anti-christ preparing for war. He is going about asking for men and for assistance from the nations under his influence. The dragon, beast, and false prophet will have the ability to do works that will convince men to become part of their one-world government as well as joining them in battle.

Revelation 16, 13-16: (13) "And I saw three unclean spirits like frogs *come* out of the mouth of the <u>dragon</u>, and out of the mouth of the <u>beast</u>, and out of the mouth of the false prophet. (14) For they are the spirits of <u>devils</u>, working miracles, *which* go forth unto the kings of the earth and of the whole world, to gather them to the battle of that great day of God Almighty. (15) **Behold, I come as a thief. <u>Blessed</u>** *is* **he that watcheth, and keepeth his garments, lest he walk naked, and they see his shame.** (16) And he gathered them together into a place called in the He'brew <u>tongue</u> Ar-ma-ged'don." (KJV)

This gives us insight about the three main leaders of the one-world government and who is influencing or empowering them. They have to travel around to many nations to recruit people to join them for the upcoming battle. Again, this is John's whole world not our whole world.

In this verse God is giving directions for us to follow.

Revelation 16, 15: "**Behold, I come as a thief. <u>Blessed</u>** *is* **he that watcheth, and keepeth his garments, lest he walk naked, and they see his shame.**" (KJV)

Our Father in heaven is the one speaking to us here. He is telling us of His soon coming judgment of all people. He is warning us to keep our garments pure so we will not be exposed and put to shame. Just to clarify, this passage is not speaking of keeping our clothes clean.

The garments He is referring to are the garments of righteousness worn by God's people. The people who are mentioned in this passage are not the ones who will partner with the ant-christ and therefore have his mark. It is not possible for them to have garments of righteousness if they carry his mark.

If God is addressing people who have the ability to keep their garments, then they cannot be the people and nations who have joined the anti-christ and the one-world government that are going against Israel. The people that were being solicited by the dragon, beast, and the false prophet are already partnered with them. Again, this passage cannot be referring to the whole world as we know it.

Our Father in heaven would not bother to make a statement like this, if everyone on the earth had taken the mark. If they had, they would be doomed to suffer the same fate that the anti-christ will suffer. They would have exposed their nakedness and we would be able to see their shame. This suggests that there are people in the world, at this time, who have not taken the required mark and are not part of the one-world government.

We need to heed all the warnings our Heavenly Father is giving us in His book. We must seek to do our part in ensuring we, and the people we love, do not give in to the evil that exists during this time.

These verses describe in detail what the people who join the one-world government will be required to do.

> Revelation 13, 16-18: (16) "And <u>he</u> causeth all, both small and great, rich and poor, free and bond, to receive a mark in their right hand, or in their foreheads: (17) And that no man might buy or sell, save he that had the mark, or the name of the beast, or the number of his name. (18) Here is wisdom. Let him that hath understanding count the number of the beast: for it is the number of a man; and his number *is* <u>Six hundred three-score *and* six</u>." (KJV)

This is the description of a physical mark (666). This mark will be a requirement that must be on the bodies of all people and a symbol that is a part of the governing practices of all the nations that join in with the anti-christ. These people will be so oppressed and under so much control by this government, that without this symbol they will not even be able to purchase or sell anything!! This is God's warning to us; we must not do anything that will connect us in any way, to this evil government.

The following verses will give you the clarity needed to understand how God feels about anyone, or any nation, that chooses to join or become part of that one-world government ruled by the anti-christ. We do not want to be on the wrong side of these battles which appear to be in the near future.

In these next 2 verses we are also told of the price people will pay for taking the mark of the beast.

> **Revelation 14, 9-11:** (9) "A third <u>angel</u> followed them and said in a loud voice: If anyone worships <u>the beast</u> and his image and receives his mark on the forehead or on the hand, (10) he, too, will drink of the wine of God's fury, which has been poured full strength into the cup of his wrath. He will be tormented with burning sulfur in the presence of the holy angels and of the Lamb. (11) And the smoke of their torment rises forever and ever. There is no rest day or night for those who worship the beast and his image, or for anyone who receives the mark of his name." (NIV)

This chapter and these verses are quite clear about what the consequences are for giving into the pressure these evil people will place upon mankind during this time.

If you take the mark upon your body, do his bidding, or worship the beast you will suffer the same fate that is reserved for the dragon, beast, and the false prophet. You will be tormented in a fiery pit with no rest for all eternity. I personally do not want to go there. Whatever price I must pay on this earth, will be a picnic compared to the alternative. God didn't hide that part from our understanding!!!

Here is more information given to us about this time in Revelation:

> Revelation 14, 12: "Here is the patience of the saints: here *are* they that keep the commandments of God, and the faith of Je'sus." (KJV)

Here again, God is addressing the fact that there are Christians present during this time mentioned in the Bible.

They did not accept the easy way out and join in with the evil leaders that want to control everything and everyone. This is speaking of people who have faith in Jesus. Remember, the Jewish people will not be faithful to Jesus at this time.

Farther along in this book you will see that God holds the same judgment toward nations as He places upon individuals. Our Father loves us. That is why He wants us not only to know about the troubles that are coming, but He also wants us to know how to overcome those problems. He wants us to know what will happen to us if we decide to do the wrong things.

Here is more evidence that Christians are here during this time.

> Revelation 13, 7-8: (7) "And it was given unto him to make war with the saints, and to overcome them: and power was given him over

all kindreds, and tongues, and nations. (8) And all that dwell upon the earth shall worship him, whose names are not written in the book of life of the Lamb slain from the foundation of the world." (KJV)

In this biblical quote, it clearly states that there will be people on the earth during this time, that will be saved and not under the control of the one-world government. It states that all men that dwell on this earth shall worship the anti-christ except the people whose names are written in the Lamb's Book of Life.

God is emphasizing the importance of this statement by adding this verse.

Revelation 13, 9: "If any man have an ear, let him hear." (KJV)

Because of this statement, we know God wants us to pay attention to what was just said.

In this quote, it clearly states that there will be people on the earth, during this time, that will be saved and not under the control of the one-world government. It states that all men that dwell on the earth shall worship the anti-christ except the Christians whose names are written in the Lamb's book.

Remember, there are many different people, tribes, and nationalities written in the Lamb's book. The common thread that connects us all together is, we have accepted Jesus as our personal Savior and are trying to do His work on this earth.

Now, let us look into some of the biblical quotes from Daniel that I believe really help to back the information I was given. They help support the fact that the beast and the anti-christ do not have as much control over the whole world, as implied in John's account, given to us in Revelation. God told us He hid much of what we would need to know to be able to survive this troubled time, until now when it will be needed.

This verse states there are areas, even in the lands described in the Bible, that are not under the control of the beast. Daniel speaks of these areas here:

> Daniel 11, 41: "He shall enter also into the glorious land, and many *countries* shall be overthrown: but these shall escape out of his hand, *even* E'dom, and Mo'ab, and the chief of the children of Am'mon." (KJV)

This passage refers to specific areas and people the anti-christ was not able to overpower from the lands both Daniel and John wrote about. It appears the anti-christ, backed by satan, will not overtake everyone he attempts to conquer after all. I don't know how you feel about that but I am glad to hear it!

This verse identifies another area that will escape the anti-christ's control and is actually coming to battle against the beast and to protect Israel.

> Daniel 11, 30: "For the ships of Chit'tim shall come against him: therefore he shall be grieved, and return, and have indignation against the holy <u>covenant</u>: so shall he do; he shall even return, and have intelligence with them that forsake the holy <u>covenant</u>." (KJV)

In this passage, the Jewish people are referred to as – the holy covenant.

This verse shows us that the anti-christ is mad about the fact that he and his followers are stopped from attacking Israel. The retreat they were forced to make has only made him even more determined to overtake God's chosen people. It tells us that after a time, the anti-christ returns to negotiate his way into getting the Jewish people to accept him.

There must be Jews who are forsaking the covenant or are deceived by the anti-christ to allow this to happen. I say this because the Bible is using the same words, "the holy covenant" to describe the people that the anti-christ is going against as well as with the ones he is trying to negotiate with – which are the Jewish people in Israel.

In other words, when war causes some of the areas that the beast and anti-christ do not control to rise up against their attack, the anti-christ will be forced to back off from his direct attack against Israel. That verse also tells us, after a time, this evil leader will then return and attempt to overcome God's chosen people through negotiations. I am sure, also with promises that he does not intend to keep – a typical tactic our enemy uses.

This next verse is very interesting to me as this is where, I believe, we are injected into the narrative Daniel is giving us.

> Daniel 11, 44-45: (44) "But reports from the east and the north will alarm him, and he will set out in a great rage to destroy and annihilate many. (45) He will pitch his royal tents between the seas at the beautiful holy mountain. Yet he will come to his end, and no one will help him." (NIV)

It is interesting that no one come to help him.

If the beast has so much control over all the nations, why then should we expect to see any nation fail to help him? If he is in control of all nations, he should have plenty of people backing him. This is where things really begin to break down for the belief that everyone and every nation is controlled by the anti-christ in these end times.

This also implies that the beast will accelerate his efforts and go out with a fury to accomplish his goal in fear of what the east and the north will do. These unnamed areas suggests that Daniel did not know the names of these two locations or of the people. At the same time, this news when given to the anti-christ disturbs him so much that he intensifies the attacks in hopes of quickly winning.

This also shows us that he will not even have control over the areas partnering with him because it states no one comes to help him. Daniel's information shows us that the beast will not have as much control over the rest of the world as implied by John.

My understanding is that these unknown areas, mentioned in the above verses, scared those partnering nations away from helping him. How then can we believe that he has complete control over all the areas of the earth, especially those areas which are not mentioned in God's word?

These passages seem to give us the idea that the anti-christ is having a difficult time accomplishing his purpose and he has to work hard at keeping everything under his control. It appears that the anti-christ has some scrambling to do in order to muster up his army and his focus appears to be divided. He is not allowed to devote his whole focus on destroying Israel. This sounds like the beast has some serious opposition outside of Israel.

After everything is said and done, the anti-christ certainly seems to have a lot less control over his domain than is implied in Revelation. How can we assume that all the earth is controlled by the one-world government, if even the areas described in the Bible were not all controlled by the anti-christ?

This should start to make more sense to us today and give us some direction as to what is expected of us. We must be sure America does not join in with the evil that is behind what is starting to happen today.

These next 2 verses are referring to the fact that many things about this prophecy will be revealed in the time of the end. God, in His goodness, wants to protect His people from the problems and worries that are not necessary for them to go through. That is why our Heavenly Father sealed the understanding of the end times until it would be needed. He had this information saved so His children, living during this time, can be shown what is necessary for us to know.

Daniel did not receive the answer to his request from God.

> Daniel 12, 8-9: (8) "And I heard, but I understood not: then said I, O my Lord, what *shall be* the end of these *things*? (9) And he said, Go thy way, Dan'iel: for the words *are* closed up and <u>sealed</u> till the time of the end." (KJV)

This statement in Daniel is easy for us to understand.

God's intensions are very clear. He gave Daniel instructions on what God wanted him to do. Our Heavenly Father was protecting Daniel and all those many generations to follow. They did not need to be burdened with the understanding and what the next steps would be because they did not need to make them. Remember, God will give us what we need to know one step at a time.

This next verse puts emphasis on our keeping ourselves pure and sanctified:

> Daniel 12, 10: "Many shall be purified, and made white, and tried; but the wicked shall do wickedly: and none of the wicked shall understand; the wise shall understand." (KJV)

One of the things this passage shows us is that both God's children and the wicked will be left during this period of time.

The message Daniel is sharing with us indicates that we will have choices to make that will require us to stand up for what we believe in. We always have the right to choose what we will do in this short life we are given on this earth. God wants us to know what will happen if we go along with the direction the evil in this world wants us to take.

He wants us to choose to stand strong and defend what He has given us. The fact that the Christians and the wicked are both present during this time makes more sense to me than what I have heard about the end times before. God loves us so much that He wants everyone in heaven with Him. The Bible tells us that.

Why would our Father leave His earth void of all God's children who can show His love and share His word with the people who have not made the decision to accept Jesus yet? It makes more sense that God would leave Christians here to help influence the rest of the world.

Do you really think God would allow an entire period in time to be void of the saving influence of the preaching and the practice of His word? God wants us to continue living the life we are taught to live from His word, the Bible. We are to be a light in dark places and we are to show His love through the way we live our lives. He expects us to stand strong against the evil forces that are even now trying to drag us into a one-world government. We need to seek understanding about the wisdom that God is now and will be pouring out on this earth, so we will not be deceived.

Some of the things spoken of in the Bible about the time of the end have not taken place as of yet.

These next 2 verses give us insight into what needs to happen.

> Daniel 12, 11-12: (11) "From the time that the daily sacrifice is abolished and the abomination that causes desolation is set up, there will be 1,290 days. (12) Blessed is the one who waits for and reaches the end of the 1,335 days." (NIV)

This passage from God's word is giving us an important time frame that has not occurred yet.

The Bible states here that these sacrifices will be resumed and once again be forbidden. After that, there will occur an incident that will start the clock to a very important countdown. That is when we need to pay even more attention to what is happening in Israel. This verse speaks of the time when offenses against God will no longer be tolerated. That incident must be very upsetting to God as it starts the countdown described here.

The daily sacrifices, that are required by the Jewish Old Testament laws, have not begun to be practiced again in Israel as of yet. So, these things are not set to happen until the sacrifices are once again stopped. It states here that when the sacrifices are stopped and the abomination is set up, that is when the countdown will begin. The difference between 1,290 and 1,335 days is 45 days. I know I do not want to be in that area during this 45-day period because of what God said in these verses. He is congratulating the people who make it through that period of time.

Even though this part of the warning God is giving us has not occurred, we can see things starting to line up with what He is saying to us. We need to ensure that all people, especially Americans, are aware of the warnings the Bible gives us. Then we can prevent our nation, and the people we care about, from being dragged into the influence of the anti-christ and under the control of the beast. I say Americans, as our nation is not specifically mentioned and my desire is for America to complete the job God has created for us to do.

If you are under the control of the anti-christ, you are forced to take his mark and worship him. The people that join the one-world government must take the mark of the beast. If you take that mark, the Bible clearly states that you cannot enter heaven.

The United States of America, and the people living in it, are not to become (in any way offered to us) a part of the one-world government that will be controlled by the anti-christ. God does not want us taking any part in the evil behind that group of nations. We, Christians, must not allow that to happen.

These verses are speaking of the anti-christ's followers and of his army.

> Revelation 6, 15-17: (15) "And the kings of the earth, and the great men, and the rich men, and the chief captains, and the mighty men, and every <u>bondman</u>, and every free man, hid themselves <u>in</u> the dens and in the rocks of the mountains; (16) And said to the mountains and rocks, fall on us, and hide us from the face of Him that sitteth on the throne, and from the <u>wrath</u> of the Lamb: (17) For the great day of His <u>wrath</u> is come; and who shall be able to stand?" (KJV)

This passage is quite clear. It is describing the different types of people that have aligned themselves with the anti-christ and the beast's army. It mentions that all of them, will be impacted by the return of Jesus in all His glory to save our earth and His people. No one, no matter what their rank is, will be spared.

The mention of bondman indicates that some of the men in servitude or that are in the army, were forced or required to submit. Even though these bondmen were not totally free, they still had free will and could have refused to submit or take that required mark.

Everyone has a choice and we are responsible for the decisions we make, every day. We must be sure those decisions line up with what God wants us to do. Because God will hold us responsible for our choices, we need to consider the paths we take and the decisions we make very carefully. If we find ourselves going the wrong way or making bad decisions – we need to repent and ask forgiveness in Jesus's name.

This is another warning we are given. It is emphasized in this passage because the bondmen suffered the same as the ones who chose freely. The statement "...fall on us, and hide us from the face of Him that sitteth on the throne, and from the <u>wrath</u> of the Lamb:" tells us, at this point, they all realize that God is backing Jesus and that they are defeated.

We have been shown the climax of what God has planned to do to restore His world to what He gave man to take care of. We must not be on the side that goes against His will. What we allow the enemy to do to our nation, and the people in it, will be held against us. We must do our part to keep America safe from what is foretold to us in God's word.

I hope I have been able to show you how the Bible indicates that the anti-christ will not be in as much control as some people think. The biblical scriptures mentioned and many others, tell us how much God cares about what happens to us. Our loving Father would have a place of safety for His people during the time spoken of in Revelation.

This information is not meant to cause fear, worry, or stress. It is to give us peace and the knowledge we need to make sure we can stop the evil behind what we see happening now. We must prevent the people who are supporting the push to force America into joining this world government, from accomplishing anything they are trying to do that would force us into that system.

It is not in God's plans that we abandon our responsibilities and give up America to be controlled by the anti-christ or to join that one-world government. In fact, we are to help protect Israel from the destruction planned for it.

# THE JUDGMENT OF NATIONS

God makes a way for His people. He defends, provides, and protects His faithful ones. We are individually judged for our actions. We know this because it is spoken of in many parts of the Bible. We are also told that God does judge nations, as a whole, for the actions taken by them as well. The Bible states that not all nations will be judged the same. Some nations will enter the kingdom prepared for His faithful ones.

If this is true, then not all nations will join the one-world government because if they do join, they must take the mark of the beast to be a part of that system. God's word states that if you take that mark, you cannot enter heaven. That alone makes it impossible for the whole world to be controlled by the anti-christ.

There will be consequences nations will have to suffer if they become part of the one-world government or the attacks against Israel. The description of the disasters in Revelation 8, do not cover the entire earth. The disasters only destroy about one third of the area described in the Bible.

In these following verses God is showing John what will happen to this area during these end times.

> Revelation 8, 8-12: (8) "And the second angel sounded, and as it were a great mountain burning with fire was cast into the sea: and the third part of the sea became blood; (9) And the third part of the creatures which were in the sea, and had life, died; and the third part of the ships were destroyed. (10) And the third angel sounded, and there fell a great star from heaven, burning as it were a lamp, and it fell upon the third part of the rivers, and upon the fountains of waters. (11) And the name of the star is called Wormwood: and the third part of the waters became wormwood; and many men died of the waters, because they were made bitter. (12) And the fourth angel sounded, and the third part of the sun was smitten, and the third part of the moon, and the third part of the stars; so as the third part of them was darkened, and the day shone not for a third part of it, and the night likewise." (KJV)

Everything John is describing that he saw in his visions could be exactly as it is stated or not.

Remember, John was limited in his descriptions to us, by his understanding of what he is looking at. The star he is speaking of could be from bombings, modern-day warfare (nuclear or not), a meteor falling to earth, or it could be something we have not developed yet. Whatever it is that John was looking at, by his own words, is only affecting at most two thirds of the world described by him in the Bible. No matter what it is that is causing this damage, it does not describe judgment sent to the whole world. This part of the vision is focusing on an area that covers only a part of John's whole earth.

This judgment will leave most of the rest of our planet untouched by its damage. There will be water in parts of the world that will be safe. God's faithful children, who are in the nations that are not involved in the attempt to overtake the Jewish people and are not part of this one-world government, will be protected. Add to this, at least one third of the land mass of John's world will not suffer what is described in the end-time battle. That is a lot of land!! Christians that are still here during this period of time described in Revelation, will have a place that will be a safe haven for us.

These verses are reference to the fact that not all nations will be judged the same.

> Matthew 25, 31-32: (31) "**When the Son of man shall come in His glory, and all the holy angels with Him, then shall He sit upon the throne of His glory:** (32) **And before Him shall be gathered all nations; and He shall separate them one from another, as a shepherd divideth** his **sheep from the goats:**" (KJV)

This is referring to Jesus conducting the end-time judgment on nations. The sheep nations are the nations that have pleased God and kept His commandments.

These verses continue speaks of nations being judged just as people will be judged.

> Mathew 25, 33-34: (33) "**And He shall set the sheep on His right hand, but the goats on the left. (34) Then shall the King say unto them on His right hand, Come, ye blessed of My Father, inherit the kingdom prepared for you from the foundations of the world:**" (KJV)

The sheep nations will not have to suffer the punishment that the nations who had joined with the beast will have to suffer. How interesting.

The nations on the left hand are those nations that cooperated with the beast or joined that evil one-world government. They are referred to as goats. The following verse gives us more information about Jesus's judgment.

> Matthew 25, 41: "**Then shall He say also unto them on the left hand, Depart from Me, ye cursed, into everlasting fire, prepared for the devil and his angels:**" (KJV)

These nations have committed evil to the point that they must be sent into the fiery pit which was prepared for the devil and his angels.

The fact that Jesus is speaks of nations receiving the inheritance of God's faithful ones makes me wonder – if the kingdom spoken of here may still be on this newly restored earth. It also states that Jesus and His angels came to that place, we didn't go to where He was. Just a thought I had. It does show that God will judge nations like He judges individuals.

When He speaks of the judgment of nations being nations as sheep and goats, this tells us that not all nations have followed the anti-christ, have taken his mark, or joined in with the beast. If all nations are under the control of the anti-christ, then all nations would have to take his mark on their hand or their forehead. This would make all nations considered goats – no nation could then be considered a sheep. There must be nations existing during this time that are not members of the one-world government and are not controlled by the anti-christ.

If you become part of that one-world government, you must take the identifying mark. God called some nations sheep so this implies that some nations will not join this one-world government. If you factor into our biblical understanding this knowledge, it changes your thinking about our nation's role in the end-time picture.

The judgment described in Revelation 8, will leave most of the rest of this planet untouched by its damage. God's faithful children, who are in the nations which are not involved in this attempt to overtake the Jewish people in Israel, will be protected. We that are still here during this period of time, described in Revelation, will have a place to stay that will be safe. We need to ensure that our nation, America, does not aligned itself with what the anti-christ intends to do.

God does pay attention to what we do collectively as a nation.

> Psalm 9, 16-17: (16) "The Lord is known *by* the judgment *which* He executeth: the wicked is <u>snared</u> in the work of his own hands (17) The wicked shall be turned into hell, *and* all the nations that forget God." (KJV)

We do not want to be numbered as a nation that forgot God.

America was set aside and saved to be a refuge for God's children, both Christians and Jews, during the end-time struggles. We are one of the few nations existing today which can truly be that self-sufficient, self-reliant, and self-supportive nation. We are strong and independent enough to resist the control of any other nation. America can also defend smaller nations who do not want to join that one-world government. Stating all this is only true if we continue to be the nation God started us out being.

I am not debating when, where, or how often God will decide to take His children home collectively or be raptured as many Christians like to refer to these events. God is sovereign and can do whatever He decides to do. I know the rapture will happen at least once because the Bible says it will happen. So when or how often it occurs is debatable, but what is not debatable is the fact that during the time of the end, there will be Christians present on the earth.

The loving nature of our Heavenly Father is one of protection for His faithful ones. So, if you are here or if you are raptured before all this happens is a personal matter. God will decide who goes and who stays. The important part of the whole picture is, some of His faithful believers in Jesus Christ will be here during that time to be used by Him. It is our job to ensure there is a safe place for them to live in during these troubled times.

What we allow to happen today, especially politically, will head our nation in the direction God wants us to take or head us down the path of destruction. We must not ignore our responsibilities. If we neglect to save America and leave before all this takes place – what kind of a nation will we be leaving behind for our children to deal with? We, God's people, both Christians and Jews have the responsibility to ensure we do not join that one-world government.

# AMERICA'S DESTINY

I had asked God for insight in America's part in Revelation for several years without getting any definite answer. America is my nation. I am an intercessor. Praying for my country is a practice I do as part of my daily life and will continue to do so as long as there is breath in my body. Here is what happened that caused me to write this book – America's Role in Revelation.

In the spring of 2009, I was so upset about what was happening to our nation and to us, the people living in this country, that I went on a four and one-half month liquid fast with intercession. After completing the fast, I received insight from God about the question of America's role in the coming days as well as insight about what God wants from us in this end-time period.

Let me clarify something: I was not fasting for the answer received. I was fasting for God to get involved in what was happening, at that time, to us and to our nation. Our Heavenly Father's response to me was much more than what was expected and it took some time seeking clear direction before I took any action upon His response.

Fasting and prayer are often required before important events are unfolded to God's people. Here is an example in Daniel of a similar action.

> Daniel 10, 2-5: (2) "At that time I, Daniel, mourned for three weeks. (3) I ate no choice food; no meat or wine touched my lips; and I used no lotions at all until the three weeks were over. (4) On the twenty-fourth day of the first month, as I was standing on the bank of the great river, the Tigris, (5) I looked up and there before me was a man dressed in linen, with a belt of the finest gold around his waist." (NIV)

This shows us what Daniel did to receive an answer to his request. He received the answer to his appeal to God when he added the sacrifice of fasting and prayer.

After these verses, Daniel goes on to describe the encounter with the man (or angel) who came to him. Daniel continues to say:

> Daniel 10, 7-8: (7) "I, Daniel, was the only one who saw the vision; the men with me did not see it, but such terror overwhelmed them that they fled and hid themselves. (8) So, I was left alone, gazing at this great vision; I had no strength left, my face turned deathly pale and I was helpless." (NIV)

Here is a description of a person, Daniel, receiving a message from God.

Daniel, just like John experienced, had some physical consequences from his encounter with a heavenly messenger. In this passage Daniel was fasting and seeking the Lord for three weeks right before God revealed the vision to him.

Many things that God needs to share with His people require someone, on this earth, to do something in preparation to receive from God what He wants to give us. The obedient servant must take time to seek the Lord. Often fasting and intercession are required in order to receive the information or blessing that God wants us to have. You can see here that God responds to our requests – especially when a sacrifice is attached to those requests.

If you want something from God and will offer up prayer and sacrifice, this alone will not guarantee that you will receive what you are asking for from God. You also must be in good standing with Him and keep the faith needed to receive your answer. God decides when, were, and who He will bless for many reasons. That is were spending time with He is so beneficial for helping us understand His way of doing things.

I will share with you a condensed version of what God gave to me. His reply was that He had saved this land called America, from being developed until this end time to create a special nation. Our Heavenly Father wants America to be a protected place for both Christians and Jews during the end-time scenario spoken of in the Bible.

We are to continue to protect smaller nations – those nations that will reject joining the one-world government. God intended for us to stay a self-sufficient, independent, self-supporting nation dedicated to Him and His work on this earth. God did not save America for us to allow it to become a part of the one-world government described in Revelation. He expects our nation to defend and protect Israel during these end times.

After a period of several months of seeking clarity about what was shown, I then started seeking His direction as to what was to be done with this information. The result of all this is what is written in this book. My hope is that everyone will have a better understanding of what is happening right now.

Our nation, the United States of America, was established July 4, 1776 about 248 years ago. It was mainly established as a biblically-based nation by people seeking freedom to worship God. We prospered and grew quickly as long as we kept God and the Bible as the basis for the governing of our nation and the education of our children.

We, God's people, have allowed the leaders in our government to abandoned the Godly principles established from the foundation of this nation. This depletion of His principles has also occurred in our schools and our court systems as well. Too many of us, Christians, are standing by while the enemy is attacking all areas of prosperity and protection that our founding fathers put in place to protect us. Do you really think that is what God wants us to do? The consequences of us doing this are mounting.

God developed America to be different from any other nation ever recorded. God set up our government to be biblically based in all forms of its governing authority. We can see His hand in many aspects of our early development. We should not have won the war against England to obtain our freedom as a nation. Even with our civil war, the side for righteousness won in that war too. The odds were against us again in the war in Texas with Mexico, but we won again.

We were on the leading edge with great advancements for our country as long as we were keeping God and His biblical principles as the basis of our way of life and the basis for the teaching in our schools. It grieves me to say, many of God's people in our nation have failed to do their part to ensure these important areas are continuing to uphold God's principles.

If you take into consideration that God made America different from any other nation, by making it a melting pot of people from many different nationalities, with a unique form of government, and founded by people who had a deep desire to serve God – people should wonder if there was a reason our Father in heaven did this.

God surely must have a plan in place for our nation. Why else would He wait so late to bring America into the picture? God saved this land from being developed by any other nation or organized group of people, until it was needed to be established by and for His people.

We really do not need anything from any other country to exist. We can produce all of the things that we need right here in our nation and in our own soil. There is much talk today about our dependence on oil from other nations and how this affects our economy. This fact is very true. We are letting other nations hold us hostage over oil prices. Why are we doing this?

We have more oil in the lands we own than is reported in the areas that we are presently buying oil from. It has been reported, this administration (for several years now) has done things to prevent our American companies from being able to produce the oil we need. Does this seem like a financially sound decision for any nation to make? Does it make much sense at all, to you, that we are doing this?

Many of the decisions that are being made for us today, by the people who have authority over us, do not match what the Bible is telling us to do. Our enemy has been chipping away, for many years now, at the very protections we take for granted.

The evil behind all that is happening in America, has already destroyed enough of those protections to try and finish the job. He intends to do this by using all his power, influence, and everything that he has control of already. It is time we, God's people, both Christians and Jews change this.

This nation was saved for a purpose and our Father in heaven expects us to keep control of what He graciously saved for us. We have sat back and allowed too much damage to occur in our nation already. The good news is – we still have time to change the direction our country is taking, but we must get involved quickly as the plans to force us into that one-world system are already in place.

This includes changing our money into a digital form which will give the government almost limitless control over it. With as much fraud and theft as we are seeing today, within our credit card system and other forms of digital usage, why would we want ALL our finances tied into a digital system that will be just as vulnerable to fraud and theft? We must not let satan take dominion of the gift God gave us – a biblically-based nation, America. A safe haven for His people.

Our country is not only capable of existing by itself without any help from other nations, we are also strong enough to help protect any smaller nation that may want to resist joining the one-world government.

If we fail to keep our nation the country God designed us to be, what other nation can take our place and be that big brother to these smaller nations who do not want to join the one-world government? There is more at stake here than just losing our country, America.

If we fail to take back our nation and reestablish the Godly principles we once had, we will have lost the ability to be the end-time influence that God saved this nation for. There is a reason why our nation was not established until this end time. We in America have an obligation to keep our country a biblically-based nation that is serving God until the day Jesus returns.

I understand that a lot of this information is different from what we have heard in the past. I tried to pack as much scripture into this book as needed, to show you how those scriptures relate to what was given to me to share with you. America does have an important role in what will shortly be happening on the earth. It is very important that we, Christians, understand our individual role in this time period.

Our Father has a job for each one of His children. He expects us to keep ourselves, our families, our cities, and our nation compliant with His laws and principles as long as we are breathing on this earth. We are to be His hands, feet, and mouthpiece to influence our surroundings and the people He gives us. We are to do our part to help make and keep America dedicated to God and His principles of life. Many of God's people living in our nation are dedicated to doing just that.

We can still say that America is the nation that is sending the message of the gospel out to the entire world more than any other nation. Many Christians in our country take part in these charitable works either personally or by supporting this effort financially. We still give to help other people and other nations when disaster hits them. Our nation is still jumping in to help defend smaller nations when trouble seems to be overwhelming those countries. Although this does go to our credit, I must tell you this is not enough.

We, God's family, have let our nation become weak through inner decay. We have stepped back and allowed to many areas in America, be taken over by the evil influences that are trying to destroy us. We, Christians, have been slow to partake in new areas of development like the movie industry, TV networks, the internet, and many other areas of advancement which were given to us for our use. God told us knowledge would increase during this time before Jesus Christ returns.

We were slow to use all these new tools to spread God's word from the onset of their development.

We have allowed these opportunities to be dominated by the wrong people. The result of our negligence has been that the wrong message has influenced not only the people who do not know God, but our very own children as well!!

Too many of God's people have stayed in our churches and allowed others to take over the protection, development, and governing of our nation. God expects us to keep our country under His influence and direction.

Jesus is showing us how He feels about us:

> Matthew 12, 47-50: (47) "Then one said unto Him, Behold, Thy mother and Thy brethren stand <u>without</u>, desiring to speak with Thee. (48) But He answered and said unto him that told Him, **Who is My mother? and who are My brethren?** (49) And He stretched forth His hand toward His disciples, and said, **<u>Behold</u> My mother and My brethren!** (50) **For whosoever shall do the will of My Father which is in heaven, the same** *is* **My brother, and sister, and mother.**" (KJV)

Jesus's family does the will of His Father in heaven. Therefore we, Christians, are expected to be Jesus' family doing God's will on this earth as long as we are here.

For too many years now Christians have believed that what is happening to our nation was foretold in the Bible. Since John said that the whole world was controlled by the anti-christ, many people assume that we in America have to become a part of that one-world government.

This belief has caused discouragement and an attitude that there is really nothing that they can do about it. Because of this belief, many Christians have chosen to do nothing to stop what is happening to our nation. It is not that they do not care about what is happening. What is stopping them from getting involved is – they do not want to do something that is going against what they believe is God's will for America.

Too many of us are counting on being raptured out of here before the real trouble starts. That may happen for some of us, but I do not see when the time the rapture will happen is clearly spelled out in God's Word. As stated before, the Bible says there will be at least one rapture and He can choose to take us up to heaven at any time He wants too. What I do see is a loving God who does not want anyone to perish or go into that fiery pit designed for the devil and his followers.

God's word shows us that both Christians and our Jewish brothers are present during the end times described in Revelation. If we have to be here anyway, I personally, would rather be in a place of protection and comfort than the alternative.

We must get actively involved and make the changes soon before it is too late. If we do not change the direction our nation and we His people are taking, we will have to pay a very painful price for too many years to come. God has never told any of His people to sit back and let evil take over the people, properties, and gifts that He, God our Father, gave us for safekeeping.

Remember, all things belong to God. He gives us wealth, people, lands, wisdom, knowledge, and advancements as He sees fit. He expects us, not only to keep what He gave us but to multiply it as well.

This parable is lengthy but very important in describing what God's expects us to do with what we are given.

> Matthew 25, 14-29: (14) "**Again, it will be like a man going on a journey, who called his servants and entrusted his property to them. (15) To one he gave five talents of money, to another two talents, and to another one talent, each according to his ability. Then he went on his journey. (16) The man who had received the five talents went at once and put his money to work and gained five more. (17) So also, the one with the two talents gained two more. (18) But the man who had received the one talent went off dug a hole in the ground and hid his master's money.**
>
> (19) **After a long time, the master of those servants returned and settled accounts**

with them. (20) **The man who had received the five talents brought the other five. 'Master,' he said, 'you entrusted me with five talents. See, I have gained five more.'**

(21) **His master replied, 'Well done, good and faithful servant! You have been faithful with a few things; I will put you in charge of many things. Come and share your master's happiness!'**

(22) **The man with the two talents also came. 'Master,' he said, you entrusted me with two talents; see, I have gained two more.'**

(23) **His master replied, 'Well done, good and faithful servant! You have been faithful with a few things; I will put you in charge of many things. Come and share your master's happiness!'**

(24) **Then the man who had received the one talent came. 'Master, he said, 'I knew that you are a hard man, harvesting where you have not sown and gathering where you have not scattered seed. (25) So, I was afraid and went out and hid your talent in the ground. See, here is what belongs to you.'**

(26) **His master replied, 'You wicked, lazy servant! So, you knew that I harvest where I have not sown and gather where I have not scattered seed? (27) Well then, you should have put my money on deposit with the bankers, so that when I returned, I would have received it back with interest.'**

(28) **Take the talent from him and give it to the one who has the ten talents.** (29) **For everyone who has will be given more, and he will have an abundance. Whoever does not have, even what he has will be taken from him.** (30) **And throw that worthless servant outside, into the darkness, where there will be weeping and gnashing of teeth**." (NIV)

Jesus often told parables or stories to explain things about God, His way of doing thing, and what He expect us to do. This is a good example of that.

This parable or story Jesus told here is easy to understand. God gives to all people as He sees fit and expects us, not only to take good care of the blessings we are given, but we are to multiply them as well. If we fail to do so, even what we have been given will be taken from us.

It is understandable that some Christians will have trouble accepting everything written in this book about America and its role in these end times. This information is different from what we have heard before. There is one thing that all of us should agree upon – it is what was just shared in the above verses. We cannot allow our nation to be taken over by God's enemies. God will not judge lightly His children who allow America to fail.

I hope you understand the responsibility for saving our nation does not hinge on you believing everything that was said about our part in these end times. The Bible is clear, we must care for and multiply the gifts we are given. We ALL must do what is necessary to save our nation and reestablish God's principles. We must take back the areas we have allowed the enemy to control. America must not join that one-world government!! Here is what we can do to save our nation.

America has fallen from our position of leadership worldwide – especially during these past 3.5 years. We must turn things around if we expect to be saved from the control of the soon coming one-world government.

There are nations, at this present time in history, discussing the possibility of forming a one-world government and the structure it will take. The current weakness in our present president and the corruption in many of our leaders in Washington, are only adding fuel to this possibility. The push to establish a national and a global digital dollar is just another way for governments to gain even more control over our affairs as well as increasing their ability to monitor everything we do.

America's present condition is not what God had planned for us or for our nation. He is warning us not from being a mean controlling Father. It is from His love for us. He wants us to know what we need to do to stay protected and obedient to what will make things better for us and for our future generations.

Our Father in heaven uses us to bring about His will on this earth. It is our responsibility to follow His commands and be faithful servants of what we are given. If we fail, we will soon reap a way of life that will not return a lifestyle that many have enjoyed before. We will become like so many other nations that allowed their governments to take control of their everyday lives.

We must get involved in overseeing and participate in our government affairs. Starting with electing men and women who have a loving respect for God. They also must be willing to fight to turn our nation around and restore the biblical principles that this nation was built upon.

Law and order must be re-established and the court systems cleaned up. We have to regain control over our public school system and start teaching fundamental education with our true national history being taught once again. Teaching about our true history does include God in it.

Parental rights need to be given back to our families. It is the responsibility of God's people to take charge of what our Father has given to us. It is much better to be biblically correct than what people today are calling politically correct. Nothing is correct that is going against what God considers to be right.

America, right now, is too strong to be taken by force. Although it is very possible for this nation to fail by financial crumbling and by social-moral decline. This is happening much quicker than you think.

Everything is being set up for our financial collapse. When our debt equals the point where we cannot pay it back, within a reasonable time period, the collateral will be pulled. The paper money that our present government is rapidly making today, to pay for the ever-increasing debt we are accumulating, is connected to creditors that will need to be paid. It is not free money.

The push to establish a digital dollar will only make it much easier for the leadership in our government to collect from us, what they decide is our portion of the debt that the present leaders in Washington are building at an incredible rate!! They will have the ability to withdraw or withhold any money we will have, since it will be digitalized!! Another loss of our freedom – this time through financial control!!!

It will be much easier for you to see the current debt we have, almost minute by minute, by going to this website:

## US Debt Clock.org
http://www.usdebtclock.org/

As of the rewriting of this book – the current debt listed, at the above website, is getting too close to 35 TRILLION DOLLARS. It is rising at an alarming rate, as you will see when you visit this site. It not only gives you the amount of our nation's debt – it breaks it down to who it is going to, as well as the amount that is going to them. There is a lot more information there than before. We not only need to stop this monumental increase in our debt – we must reverse it as well.

The following statistics and website are from information in the original book. I felt it was important to keep the information in this revised version of the book. Not sure if you can get information from TresuryDirect that is broken down this way anymore. At least, I could not find it. Do you think that just might be deliberate??

# TreasuryDirect

## The Debt to the Penny and Who Holds It

https://www.treasurydirect.gov/

| Current Date | Debt Held by the Public |
|---|---|
| 04/05/10 | $8,315,716,104,736.67 |

| Intergovernmental Holdings | Total Public Debt Outstanding |
|---|---|
| $4,470,842,955,615.91 | $12,786,559,060,352.58 |

Unfortunately, we are spending more than what is being collects from us through all the different forms of taxations we are already having to pay. We need to demand our Representatives put the government on a budget just like we have to do with our own finances.

This is one reason why some people in Washington are pushing to establish a form of digital money. With a digital way to access everyone's financial accounts, it is possible for our government to decide to withdraw or freeze the money we have. This form of money also gives them the ability to see every dime we spend and what we spend it on. Our privacy will no longer exist.

If we allow the wrong people to control our government, the information they collect can be used against us for any reason they choose. Our personal finances as well as our freedoms will be very vulnerable.

Money lending usually ensures some form of collateral to allow protection of the lender's investment. The collateral for our nation's debt is all our lands, property, and we the people as chattel (bondsmen or slaves).

Do not think that the very people who are spending all this money will do anything to stop the collection of that debt! The wrong people in control will be sure to make a deal for themselves then cooperate with the lenders for the takeover, possibly even help them do it!! If we allow this to continue, there will be little choice in the matter for us, especially if they have the ability to just take money from our accounts digitally!!!

Our government has been run by too many politicians who have little or no experience in these matters and/or they are too willing to compromise to ensure the positions they currently hold will be saved for them. Too many of our social programs are put in place to keep us happy while they keep the spending going in other questionable areas. Often the money that is designated for these projects, is not spent in the way they were designed to be spent either!!

We are in trouble with our Social Security as well. (This is a good example of what was just said.) It is now paying for many of these social programs. Back when it was started, it was sold to hard working people as being a protected savings account for us when we retire. It only took about 2 years before many of the same people who promised it would be protected, had opened it up to be accessed for other things – not just for our retirement. The government keeps finding more programs to be added to deplete it. Social Security has been projected to be no longer solvent within most of our lifetimes. This also needs to be changed.

If we do not reverse the direction we are taking in this nation, we will soon be so far into debt that our lenders will have no choice but to take over this country for payment of our debts. This is all part of our enemy's plan.

For the destruction and takeover of America to happen, all we have to do is keep up this crazy spending and we will be part of that one-world government by force. Many of us will have hard choices to make if that happens. Even if some of God's children are raptured before the trouble starts, do you really think God will be pleased with what we, His family, have allowed to happen to America?

We are responsible to keep track of what our Representatives and Senators are doing in

Washington. It is their job to represent us by presenting what we want done in Congress. It is our job to let them know what we expect them to do!! We must contact our Representatives and demand they do something to cut back on this spending before it is too late.

The House of Representatives is the one responsible for overseeing the government spending. We must let them know how we feel about the runaway spending as well as the changing of our money from the paper dollar into a digital one. A digital dollar is too vulnerable to theft, can be accessed too easily by the government, and the information that is tied to it can be used against us!! It is time we made sure our Representatives are doing the job we sent them to Washington to do.

Why do you think this administration is allowing illegals to freely walk into our nation?? Why have the people behind Biden decided to spend our tax dollars on these unvetted people?? They are using our social programs to give money to these non-citizens to the tune of thousands of dollars each!! It has been reported that some illegals are even being put up in hotels with our tax dollars!!!

What do you think is the reason for this current administration's attempt to fast tracking these illegals into becoming citizens without using our well-established safeguards?? Why are they deciding to downsize our military?? What is their excuse for depleting our once well stocked weapons by leaving massive amounts of them behind in nations when we leave or by giving them away to other nations?? At the same time, threatening to withhold weapons and our help from Israel, our ally?? We need a major change in our leadership now!!!

If you are old enough to have learned our true American history, you can see that God was involved with the creation of this nation. He has plans to use this nation, especially during these end times. God will surely judge His people who have neglected to do their duty in keeping and prospering this country, that He has given us for safekeeping. If we do not stop what is currently happening in our nation – even we, His adopted children, will not be happy with the consequences that will follow.

It is not too late. We can turn around the mess our nation is in if we all do our part now. My Heavenly Father would not have me write this book if it were too late for America. We must get involved because we are not only losing the country we are living in; we are also losing our opportunity to be used mightily by God. We must take the action needed to save our nation – starting with this 2024 election.

Here is one good thing, it is much easier to learn about the people running for office today than before but we can't trust the main-stream news alone. Best to listen to good men and women who are offering information that usually won't be covered in the news, especially on main-stream media.

Many of these new outside sources are becoming very popular now. People are beginning to recognize the bias of our once trusted news stations. If you can get your information from varied sources, you stand a better chance of getting past any bias or disinformation and learn the TRUTH. We do have people, outside of the national news stations, who are willing to present the TRUTH about what is happening to our nation.

In today's world of politics, there are too many people in Washington who want to keep the direction we are going in to continue. So, we should watch to see who is saying they want to change things and after that, are being persecuted by the people in power. These individuals are usually the ones who really intend to do what they are saying!!!

These people, if they continue to fight through the persecution, are the ones you should consider voting for. At least in the 44 years of my being involved in the political process and helping to get good people elected, I find this fact to be true. The main problem I have observed, is finding someone who will fight through all that mess and still keep going!!!

I have tried by showing you through scriptures as well as by addressing some of the present and historical facts, how much God loves us and wants to protect us. Also, how truly small the area is in John's descriptions in Revelation. It is very important that we understand our role in this time period.

We, Christian and Jewish people who follow biblical principles, must start taking back the authority in our nation that we have given over to the wrong people. America does not have to be, or is it our destiny to be, a part of that one-world government. Our nation can still be the self-supporting, self-sufficient, independent nation that is separated from the end-time European based one-world government. We can exist without buying or trading with that system. God made sure of it.

What will God say to us, His children, if we let this nation fail? Will He say, "Well done, good and faithful servants?" Will He be pleased with what He sees happening in the land that He gave us to watch over and to keep safe? Is our nation in better or worse condition than the way it was given to us? We will be held accountable (good or bad) for our part in what happens during our life time. The good thing is, we still have time to change the direction America is headed.

This 2024 election is very important. It needs to be that pivotal point we must have, to restore what we have lost and bring back the Godly principles our nation was built upon. This will allow God to become more involved in prospering and protecting us once again.

It should be obvious which president is trying to restore our nation – the one that is being persecuted by government agencies, the court system, as well as main-stream media. This is the primary factor or give away you can use in your decision making to assist you in who to vote for in this election – and not just for the presidential position either!!!

It is also very important that we scrutinize the individuals we send up to Washington to represent us, so they will help him. Once they are elected, it is best to keep in touch with them to be sure they are doing what needs to be done in our nation's capital. This will make a big difference in the president's ability to accomplish, making America great again.

If people will take the time to do this, the individuals we put into all government positions will feel the pressure and vote the way we expect them too. Now we can monitor how they vote much easier than years before. This is our job. It is more important than many people realize. We do not want the consequences that will be the result of our ignoring what is going on in Washington. That has been done for too long already.

If you are having trouble believing what I am sharing with you – ask God to show you the truth. He wants us to know the truth. Fasting with prayer is also done to make sure we are getting the answer from Him and not being influenced by anyone or anything else. That is one of the reasons why I personally do it.

My hope is, that you have understood the importance of what is being shared in this book. It is vital to our future that this information is made available to as many people as possible in order for us to save our nation.

Here is the prayer that I am sending up to God for all of the people who will read this book:

In the name of Jesus, I ask you Father, to bring clarity to the minds of the people who read this book. Help them to become closer to You and discover the plan You have for their lives. Help them accomplish the tasks You need them to do and protect them from harm. Thank you, Father.

# CONCLUSION

Our Heavenly Father is a loving caring God. He has shown us that in so many ways. One example of this is how beautiful and well balanced the world is that we live in – a world He made for us. If you take time to try to discover who God really is and how much He is willing to be part of your life, you may be pleasantly surprised.

Remember, we do have an enemy that is trying to prevent that connection. The evil behind the takeover of these nations knows his destiny. His only hope is to delay that judgment day for as long as he can through destroying or postponing God's plans or, at least, by take as many of the people God loves down with him. We can't allow that evil to take control of America or of the people we care about.

God wants us to love Him back – He does not want anyone to go to hell.

> Matthew 25, 41: "**Then shall He say also unto them on the left hand, Depart from Me, ye cursed, into everlasting <u>fire</u>, prepared for the <u>devil</u> and his angels**:" (KJV)

The everlasting fire was prepared for the devil and his angels – not for us. We go there because of our own free will and because of the choices we make during the short time we have on this earth.

God gives every opportunity possible for all people to make the right decision. God loves us so much, He sent His only Son, Jesus, to die for our sins so that we can be with our Father in heaven forever and ever. All we need to do to be saved, is to ask Jesus to be our personal Lord and Savior. If we will do this, we become God's adopted children. Then we can ask God to forgive us of our sins in Jesus's name.

There is forgiveness available to everyone who will seek after Him and follow His ways. This produces a much happier life while here on the earth, with a much better eternal life for us when we leave these bodies we inhabit.

Our Heavenly Father has always provided a safe haven for His faithful people. He will do the same for the people and the nations which are faithful to Him and His word, especially in this end-time scenario.

I hope this information and realization opens up our eyes to the direction that God expects us to take. We can no longer sit back and ignore what is happening to our nation. God never intended for America to get into the shape it is in now or be a part of that soon coming one-world government.

We have an obligation to take back control and reestablish biblical principles in all areas of our country. All of us must get involved in stopping the destruction of our nation. We have allowed the enemy to establish too many strongholds in America, and we must break those holds or we will have to answer to God for our negligence. We must act quickly in order to save our nation.

I realize this is a lot of information in a small book. I also know if you seek answers, wisdom, and understanding our loving Father will show the truth to you, if you ask.

Do not worry about the outcome of your taking action to correct the mess we are in. If we step out to do the things that God asks us to do – He will assist us in making it work. It is very possible for us to recapture our nation and restore what we have lost in as little as 2 presidential elections!!!

We can reestablish all rights and privileges that we have allowed to be taken from us. We can still be the nation God intended for us to be. We still have time if we act quickly. The longer we wait the more mess we have to clean up!!! We must not wait any longer or it may end up being too late!!!

Things have been stacked up against us accomplishing this but there is still time for us to correct it. We first must contact our state officials to change the election process, to prevent any fraudulent attempts to steal it. That will allow the good people that we have voted for to be put into all government positions. There is too much corruption in our election process right now. This is critical for the 2024 election – we can not afford to give this current administration another 4 years to continue damaging our nation.

All this starts by contacting your state representatives demanding only citizens can vote, winners to be announced on election day, and Voter IDs be required for all our elections. Paper ballots, with signatures, is a good way to ensure that there is less possibility for fraud to occur.

Not long ago, paper ballots where what we used for many years and still had the winners of that election given to us on election day!! The enemy wants more time for the announcement of the winners to be given, so it will be easier for fake votes to be added into our election process. Numbers count – we all need to take action quickly to help fix it.

If we do not change the direction America is taking, our children and our future generations will suffer the most. They will live long enough to have to bear the consequences of our neglect. They will be forced to make those hard choices once these biblical prophecies start to unfold. I do not want that for my children or my grandchildren. It is always easier to stop the problems from happening rather than to try and correct them once in place.

Thank you for reading this book. My hope is that you will get others to read it so all of us can get involved in turning around the direction our nation is taking. We then will be able to elect men and women who will bring back the Godly principles that our nation was built upon.

All we need to do is stand up against the corruption we are seeing and help get good people elected into all areas of our government. We need people in our government positions who love America and are willing to fight for it. I am hoping that we can make a major dent in the control the enemy has over our country in this 2024 election.

May the blessings of our Lord Jesus always be with you and with all the people who matter to you. May God bless you, give you wisdom, and knowledge about the role you have in taking back our nation. Again, thank you for reading this book.

# Dedication Page

I dedicate this book to the Holy Spirit of God who helped me write it. I have asked Him to enlighten the readers to the truth He wants them to receive from it, just as He does when we read God's word – the Bible. Trust that He will do it.

To anyone who may have experienced difficulty understanding parts of this book, I suggest you ask the Holy Spirit to guide you and give you the insight needed. If you learn to do this, it will change your life.

My hope is, this book will inspire the readers to seek God's wisdom for their part in ensuring America fulfills her destiny in these upcoming world events.

America's Role in Revelation Revised

# About the Author

Eileen Townsend has interceded for our nation for over 50 years. She was privileged to go on several mission trips with TBN to Russia and to Israel in the 1990's. Those experiences have also given her political insight.

Her involvement in various aspects of the election process since 1980, has allowed her to influence politicians by face-to-face meetings, letters, and e-mails. She shares on several social-media sites, what our main-stream news media is neglecting to mention.

She works to restore our Constitution, our rights, privileges, and freedoms. She is the mother of 4 and Nona to 6 grandchildren. They are very important to her and she works to ensure that they stay happy, healthy, and protected from all harm.

America's Role in Revelation Revised

# America's Role in Revelation Revised

## Reference Page

King James Version                    (KJV)

New International Version          (NIV)

Treasury Direct

https://www.treasurydirect.gov/

US Debt Clock.org

http://www.usdebtclock.org/


Here are a number of scriptures that reference the early church's belief in the earth being flat:


1 Chronicles 16:30 – Psalm 75:3 – Psalm 93:1 – Psalm 96:10 – Psalm 104:5 – Job 26:10 – Job 28:24 – Job 37:3 – Isaiah 11:12 – Isaiah 45:18 – Matthew 4:8 – Revelation 7:1

America's Role in Revelation Revised

Made in the USA
Columbia, SC
01 October 2024

42736251R00070